# DISRUPTIVE BEHAVIOR DISORDERS

## MENTAL ILLNESSES AND DISORDERS

Alzheimer's Disease
Anxiety Disorders
Attention-Deficit Hyperactivity Disorder
Autism Spectrum Disorders
Bipolar Disorder
Depression
Disruptive Behavior Disorders
Drug and Alcohol Dependence
Eating Disorders
Obsessive-Compulsive Disorder
Post-Traumatic Stress Disorder
Schizophrenia
Sleep Disorders

# MENTAL ILLNESSES AND DISORDERS
## Awareness and Understanding

# DISRUPTIVE BEHAVIOR DISORDERS

## H.W. Poole

### SERIES CONSULTANT
## ANNE S. WALTERS, PhD
Chief Psychologist, Emma Pendleton Bradley Hospital

Clinical Associate Professor, Alpert Medical School/Brown University

MASON CREST

Mason Crest
450 Parkway Drive, Suite D
Broomall, PA 19008
www.masoncrest.com

© 2016 by Mason Crest, an imprint of National Highlights, Inc. All rights reserved. No part of this publication may be reproduced or transmitted in any form or by any means, electronic or mechanical, including photocopying, recording, taping, or any information storage and retrieval system, without permission from the publisher.

MTM Publishing, Inc.
435 West 23rd Street, #8C
New York, NY 10011
www.mtmpublishing.com

President: Valerie Tomaselli
Vice President, Book Development: Hilary Poole
Designer: Annemarie Redmond
Copyeditor: Peter Jaskowiak
Editorial Assistant: Andrea St. Aubin

Series ISBN: 978-1-4222-3364-1
ISBN: 978-1-4222-3368-9
Ebook ISBN: 978-1-4222-8569-5

Library of Congress Cataloging-in-Publication Data
Poole, Hilary W., author.
  Disruptive behavior disorders / by H.W. Poole.
      pages cm.
  Includes bibliographical references and index.
  ISBN 978-1-4222-3368-9 (hardback) — ISBN 978-1-4222-3364-1 (series) — ISBN 978-1-4222-8569-5 (ebook)
  1.  Behavior disorders in children—Juvenile literature. 2.  Oppositional defiant disorder in children—Juvenile literature. 3.  Conduct disorders in children—Juvenile literature.  I. Title.
  RJ506.B44P67 2016
  618.92'858—dc23
                                                                        2015006701

Printed and bound in the United States of America.


9 8 7 6 5 4 3 2

# TABLE OF CONTENTS

## Key Icons to Look for:

 **Words to Understand:** These words with their easy-to-understand definitions will increase the reader's understanding of the text, while building vocabulary skills.

 **Sidebars:** This boxed material within the main text allows readers to build knowledge, gain insights, explore possibilities, and broaden their perspectives by weaving together additional information to provide realistic and holistic perspectives.

 **Research Projects:** Readers are pointed toward areas of further inquiry connected to each chapter. Suggestions are provided for projects that encourage deeper research and analysis.

 **Text-Dependent Questions:** These questions send the reader back to the text for more careful attention to the evidence presented there.

 **Series Glossary of Key Terms:** This back-of-the-book glossary contains terminology used throughout the series. Words found here increase the reader's ability to read and comprehend higher-level books and articles in this field.

People who cope with mental illnesses and disorders deserve our empathy and respect.

(istockphoto/digitalskillet)

# Introduction to the Series

According to the National Institute of Mental Health, in 2012 there were an estimated 45 million people in the United States suffering from mental illness, or 19 percent of all US adults. A separate 2011 study found that among children, almost one in five suffer from some form of mental illness or disorder. The nature and level of impairment varies widely. For example, children and adults with anxiety disorders may struggle with a range of symptoms, from a constant state of worry about both real and imagined events to a complete inability to leave the house. Children or adults with schizophrenia might experience periods when the illness is well controlled by medication and therapies, but there may also be times when they must spend time in a hospital for their own safety and the safety of others. For every person with mental illness who makes the news, there are many more who do not, and these are the people that we must learn more about and help to feel accepted, and even welcomed, in this world of diversity.

It is not easy to have a mental illness in this country. Access to mental health services remains a significant issue. Many states and some private insurers have "opted out" of providing sufficient coverage for mental health treatment. This translates to limits on the amount of sessions or frequency of treatment, inadequate rates for providers, and other problems that make it difficult for people to get the care they need.

Meanwhile, stigma about mental illness remains widespread. There are still whispers about "bad parenting," or "the other side of the tracks." The whisperers imply that mental illness is something you bring upon yourself, or something that someone does to you. Obviously, mental illness can be exacerbated by an adverse event such as trauma or parental instability. But there is just as much truth to the biological bases of mental illness. No one is made schizophrenic by ineffective parenting, for example, or by engaging in "wild" behavior as an adolescent. Mental illness is a complex interplay of genes, biology, and the environment, much like many physical illnesses.

People with mental illness are brave soldiers, really. They fight their illness every day, in all of the settings of their lives. When people with an anxiety disorder graduate from college, you know that they worked very hard to get there—harder, perhaps, than those who did not struggle with a psychiatric issue. They got up every day with a pit in their stomach about facing the world, and they worried about their finals more than their classmates. When they had to give a presentation in class, they thought their world was going to end and that they would faint, or worse, in front of everyone. But they fought back, and they kept going. Every day. That's bravery, and that is to be respected and congratulated.

These books were written to help young people get the facts about mental illness. Facts go a long way to dispel stigma. Knowing the facts gives students the opportunity to help others to know and understand. If your student lives with someone with mental illness, these books can help students know a bit more about what to expect. If they are concerned about someone, or even about themselves, these books are meant to provide some answers and a place to start.

The topics covered in this series are those that seem most relevant for middle schoolers—disorders that they are most likely to come into contact with or to be curious about. Schizophrenia is a rare illness, but it is an illness with many misconceptions and inaccurate portrayals in media. Anxiety and depressive disorders, on the other hand, are quite common. Most of our youth have likely had personal experience of anxiety or depression, or knowledge of someone who struggles with these symptoms.

As a teacher or a librarian, thank you for taking part in dispelling myths and bringing facts to your children and students. Thank you for caring about the brave soldiers who live and work with mental illness. These reference books are for all of them, and also for those of us who have the good fortune to work with and know them.

—Anne S. Walters, PhD
Chief Psychologist, Emma Pendleton Bradley Hospital
Clinical Professor, Alpert Medical School/Brown University

# CHAPTER ONE

# BAD DAYS

 **Words to Understand**

**aggressive:** attacking or confrontational.

**context:** the particular setting or situation of an event.

**development:** how something grows or changes over time.

**disruptive:** interrupting something by causing a problem.

**impulse:** a sudden, strong desire to do something.

**psychology:** having to do with the mind.

There is a famous book you might remember from when you were younger. It's called *Alexander and the Terrible, Horrible, No Good, Very Bad Day*. It's about a boy who wakes up one morning with gum in his hair, and his day just gets worse and worse. You've probably had days like that. We all have.

Maybe you started off feeling tired and grouchy. On the bus to school, the other kids were laughing and telling jokes. The more fun they had, the worse you felt. Maybe you wanted to tell them to shut up, already.

But you didn't.

Then you got to school, and your teacher returned a test from the day before. Your grade was bad, and the teacher wrote something mean like, "Try harder next time!" But you did try! It wasn't your fault the questions were so hard. Maybe you felt like ripping the paper into pieces and shouting, "How about *you* try harder to write a better test!"

But you didn't.

When you got home, you found that your little brother had smashed a model rocket you were working on, or maybe he got ice cream on your comic books, or maybe he just wouldn't stop bugging you. Although you love your brother, something in you wanted to punch him as hard as you could.

But you didn't do that, either.

Why didn't you do those things? Why not just act however you want?

## Impulse Control

You probably didn't do those things for two reasons. First, you knew that they would be wrong. And second, you knew they wouldn't make anything better. Being mean to your friends

**Opposite: Everyone who grows up with sisters or brothers has experienced some form of conflict with them.**

**DID YOU KNOW?**

**Experts disagree about how many kids have behavior disorders. Some studies claim that the number is as high as 1 in 5. Other experts say those studies used a definition of "behavior disorder" that is too broad. They say the number is closer to about 1 in 10.**

wouldn't make you feel less grouchy. Making a scene in class wouldn't help your grade, and it would probably get you sent to the principal's office. And even when your little brother upsets you, you don't actually want to hurt him. You were practicing good impulse control.

An impulse is an urge that occurs to you all of a sudden. There are good impulses, like suddenly deciding to do something nice for someone. There are also bad impulses, like the urge to break something or hit someone. The choice to act or not act is called impulse control. Controlling our impulses is an important part of getting along in the world.

Impulse control is pretty easy to explain, but not always easy to do. Everybody struggles with impulse control sometimes—little kids, teenagers, adults, everybody. However, the older we get, the better most of us are at controlling our bad impulses.

But that doesn't always happen. Problems with impulse control are an important aspect of disruptive behavior disorders.

## Disruptive Behavior

We all make choices about how to act. Sometimes we choose well, and other times maybe not so well. Everybody makes mistakes. But there are people who seem to make bad choices over and over again.

This happens for many reasons. Some people get so angry that they lose control. Their emotions just take over everything else. Other people can control their emotions, but they don't realize (or care) how their actions hurt others. They want to act out, so they do.

In **psychology**, this is called disruptive behavior. And ongoing problems with actions or emotions are called disruptive behavior disorders. There are a few different types. In the following chapters, we'll look at some of the most important.

## What Is Normal, Anyway?

As we said, we all have bad days. And if you are going through a difficult time—if your parents are getting divorced, or you move to a different school, or something else is

**Babies use crying and tantrums to express themselves because they don't have other skills to communicate when they are unhappy.**

## NORMAL IN DIFFICULT PLACES

The definition of *normal behavior* involves more than just a person's age. It also has to do with where and how a person lives.

Unfortunately, lots of kids do not live in safe places. They might share their home with someone who has a violent temper. Or there might be gangs and crime in their neighborhood. For those kids, it may seem normal to be more aggressive than other kids. They have seen adults around them behave that way. You might even say that aggressive behavior is expected in their environments. These kids might need more help learning how to handle their anger in a positive way. For them, the definition of "normal" is very different than for kids who grow up feeling safe.

wrong—you might have more than one bad day in a row. So how do you tell the difference between regular bad days and a disorder?

The truth is, it's not always easy to know. But one big factor involves whatever is considered normal for a specific person's age and context. Now, *normal* is a strange word because it means different things to different people. What is normal for you might not be normal for someone else. But in general, we do know some basic things about normal human behavior.

For example, it is normal for a three-year-old to have a tantrum. Maybe little Emma didn't want to eat her peas, so she threw them on the floor. Emma's behavior is disruptive, but it's normal in terms of her development. But if Emma is still throwing food when she's ten, that might not be normal. By that age, most of us have learned other ways to act when we're upset.

But even then, we can't be sure. Some kids take longer to learn certain skills. There might be a physical or psychological reason why a tantrum might be normal for Emma. No behavior checklist applies to all people all the time. Whether or not someone has a behavior disorder depends partly on what is normal for *that specific person's* development.

## How Long Has This Been Going On?

Here's another example. Teenagers often get mad at their parents. They almost always want more freedom than their parents will give them. So if Dad says, "No, Jackson, you can't have the car keys," it's quite normal for Jackson to be angry. He might shout or stomp up to his room. Maybe he'll text a friend to report what a jerk his dad is. But what if Jackson

**The teen years involve a desire for independence. This makes some conflict between teens and their parents nearly inevitable.**

smashes all the windows in the car? Or what if he just takes the car anyway? That's definitely disruptive behavior.

But that does not not necessarily mean that Jackson has a disruptive behavior disorder. One bad night—even a *really* bad night that involves stealing Dad's car—does not equal a disorder. Instead, doctors look for similar behavior over time. So a second aspect of behavior disorders is a pattern—more than just one event. It's many similar events that happen again and again.

**Arguments happen. We might not like it, but conflict is a part of life. But some people seem to be in constant conflict with everyone. Disruptive behavior disorders involve a pattern of conflict, not just the occasional argument.**

## I'm Making Us Miserable

A third aspect of behavior disorders is the effect they have on the person's life. In the Emma and Jackson examples, nobody involved was very happy at the time. But if everyone soon calmed down and started getting along, everything is probably fine.

Behavior disorders affect the person, his family, and his friends in very negative ways. They hurt the person's ability to succeed at school or work. And they often make the person who has the disorder very unhappy. The person might *say* otherwise—she'll say that she is fine, and that it's everybody else who has the problem. But, in general, having a disruptive behavior disorder is a very lonely thing.

The next chapters will talk about specific disorders. Then we'll discuss how people with these problems can get better.

## Text-Dependent Questions

1. What is an impulse? How do impulses affect our behavior?
2. Name some examples of disruptive behavior that might be expected for a certain stage in someone's development.
3. What are some of the factors doctors consider when deciding if someone has a behavior disorder?

## Research Project

Find out more about child development and impulse control. How do young kids learn impulse control, and what can they do to get better at it? Make a list of things kids might do when they lack impulse control—these can be anything from interrupting others to having tantrums to eating unhealthy food. What are some techniques to help improve impulse control? (You might start at parenting web sites, or a site hosted by *Psychology Today* called "Psych Basics: Self-Control," available at www.psychologytoday.com/basics/self-control.)

# CHAPTER TWO

# PROBLEMS WITH EMOTIONS

**Words to Understand**

**bipolar disorder:** a mental disorder involving extreme emotional highs and lows.

**intermittent:** something that happens on occasion, not constantly.

**oppositional:** being against someone or something.

**ranting:** speaking or shouting for long periods in an aggressive way.

**trigger:** something that causes a particular reaction to happen.

**vindictive:** purposefully mean, especially to "get back" at someone.

Two disruptive behavior disorders stem from a lack of emotional control. *Intermittent explosive disorder* involves a person getting so angry that he is no longer in control of what he is saying or doing. Meanwhile, *oppositional defiant disorder* involves large amounts of anger being directed at others, especially authority figures.

## Intermittent Explosive Disorder

People with intermittent explosive disorder have aggressive impulses that they can't resist. They can go from calm to aggressive in a very short period of time. Their rages can be verbal (shouting, screaming, ranting) or they can be physical (breaking things, starting fights).

**Kids who bully other kids might have a type of disruptive behavior disorder.**

## SYMPTOMS OF INTERMITTENT EXPLOSIVE DISORDER

Intermittent explosive disorder involves uncontrolled rages that

- are out of proportion to situation,
- happen at least twice a week for at least two months,
- may result in physical injury to self or others,
- may result in damage to property, and
- can't be explained by any other physical or mental condition.

What is important is that the actions of someone with intermittent explosive disorder are out of proportion with the situation. For example, some of us are quite competitive when we play games, and we might get upset if we lose. But the person with intermittent explosive disorder might start screaming, overturn the table, break the game, or even threaten the person who won.

Also important is that these kinds of rages can be caused by other emotional or physical problems. Someone with **bipolar disorder** (covered in another book in this series) might also lose emotional control in this way. So might a person with a drug or alcohol problem. But if no other issues can explain the rages, a doctor might diagnose intermittent explosive disorder.

Although aggression and violence are common in our society, intermittent explosive disorder is fairly rare. It occurs in men more often than women. It seems to crop up in childhood and become worse as a person gets older.

## Oppositional Defiant Disorder

Oppositional defiant disorder (ODD) is the most common disruptive behavior disorder. Like people with intermittent explosive disorder, people with ODD get angry easily. But the anger of people with ODD is focused on authority figures. For kids, that usually means parents and teachers. Kids with ODD defy authority frequently, and they have a lot of trouble walking away from any argument. Even if the topic of the argument is unimportant, someone with ODD will keep pushing anyway. Sometimes they seem to enjoy annoying others.

**Research has found that preschool can help lower the risk of kids developing behavior disorders later in life. This might be because preschool provides lots of opportunities for little kids to practice impulse control and conflict resolution.**

Doctors don't know what exactly causes ODD. We know that symptoms usually show up in childhood and that the disorder is slightly more common in boys than girls. Some kids do "grow out of it," but most of the time, people with ODD need some form of therapy or extra help to get better.

The common childhood problem called attention-deficit hyperactivity disorder (ADHD) can sometimes occur alongside ODD. It's also easy to confuse the two disorders. They both involve a refusal to follow instructions, but one is deliberate and one isn't. Parents and teachers have to figure out if a child is defying instructions on purpose (ODD) or if she is just easily distracted (ADHD).

One interesting aspect of ODD is that some people only show symptoms in one location. In other words, a kid with ODD might be very difficult to live with, but then be pretty well behaved at school. Or she might be hostile both at home

## SYMPTOMS OF OPPOSITIONAL DEFIANT DISORDER

Someone with ODD:

- loses his or her temper often
- is angry often
- is "touchy" or easily irritated
- argues frequently, especially with authority figures
- refuses to follow instructions or rules
- blames others for mistakes
- annoys others on purpose
- is **vindictive** regularly

## PROBLEM-SOLVING SKILLS

Some people think that ODD is a result of some mental abilities that haven't yet developed. Those skills are grouped under the broad heading of "problem solving." So children with ODD need to learn new ways to solve problems. But their thinking skills might be slower to develop, making that process harder.

and school, but not to her friends on the soccer team. The most severe cases of ODD involve the person being hostile in all situations. But many times, specific situations seem to trigger the disruptive behavior. This is why a big part of ODD therapy involves learning what those triggers are and making a plan to handle them when they appear.

### Text-Dependent Questions

1. How are the two disorders discussed in this chapter similar? How are they different?
2. What are the symptoms of intermittent explosive disorder?
3. What are the symptoms of oppositional defiant disorder?

### Research Project

Everyone gets angry sometimes. But anger can be constructive (that is, anger is used to make a situation better) or destructive (that is, anger just makes a situation worse). Research the difference between constructive and destructive anger. Write down some examples of each. How might that destructive anger be made more constructive? (To get started, you might consult the sources listed in the Further Reading section.)

# CHAPTER THREE

# PROBLEMS WITH BEHAVIOR

**Words to Understand**

**empathy:** sharing the feelings of another person.

**norm:** an accepted standard.

**violate:** to break or go against something.

The last chapter discussed disorders involving angry feelings that lead to difficult behavior. There are other disorders that might or might not involve angry feelings, but that definitely involve difficult behavior.

## Telling Right from Wrong

In chapter one, we talked about how you might (hopefully will!) choose *not* to hit your brother, because you know that it's wrong. The idea that it's wrong to hit someone is called a social norm. Social norms are unwritten rules that we all agree to follow: you don't push people, and you don't hit them; you don't take things that aren't yours; you don't pick on people

**Stealing is a violation of social norms.**

**A very rare but dangerous type of conduct disorder is *pyromania*, which involves deliberately setting fires. People with pyromania feel pleasure when they start fires and lack the impulse control to stop themselves from doing it.**

who are weaker than you. Social norms make it easier and safer to get along in the world.

When we **violate** a social norm, we usually feel bad about it afterward. If you give in to your impulse to hit your brother, he might cry. Later, when you have calmed down, you'll remember your brother crying and feel guilty that you were the cause. That's the social norm again, creeping into your head to remind you that hitting is wrong. The next time you feel that punching impulse, you may remember the guilt and, hopefully, make a better choice.

Or at least this is how social norms are meant to work. None of this is true for people with conduct disorder.

## What Is Conduct Disorder?

A person with conduct disorder often behaves in a way that violates social norms. This can involve hitting, bullying, being cruel, stealing, breaking things, hurting animals, and lying frequently. The older the person is, the more dangerous the behaviors can be—young adults with conduct disorder might commit crimes, take drugs, or run away from home. Sometimes conduct disorder can involve rages, like the ones discussed in the previous chapter. But just as often, a person with conduct disorder does not feel especially angry when he behaves aggressively. In fact, he often seems to enjoy these behaviors.

Conduct disorder can crop up when people are as young as four or five, but symptoms generally don't appear until the teen years. The disorder tends to be very difficult to treat. This is partly because there is no pill that can stop the behavior. It's also because a person with the disorder tends to push friends and family away. It's understandable that people might assume someone with a conduct disorder is just extremely unlikeable. But, in fact, the person has a mental condition—much like depression, anorexia, or other illnesses that we find more sympathetic.

## Feeling and Not Feeling

Emotions and conduct disorder are related in some confusing ways. As discussed above, someone with conduct disorder might or might not feel angry. In fact, someone with the disorder tends *not* to feel things that most people do. One of those feelings is guilt. Although it's not much fun, feeling guilty about something can be a good sign, in a way. It

**Cheating on tests is not in itself a sign of conduct disorder. However, it does violate social norms. If someone cheats a lot *and also* shows some of the other behaviors listed in these pages, it could be a sign of a larger problem.**

means that someone understands that he is responsible for something bad happening. Frequently, people with conduct disorders do not feel guilty for what they've done. They simply don't regret having hurt someone else.

Another emotion that tends to be missing is empathy. This is not true for all people with conduct disorders in all situations. But often, someone with a conduct disorder does think about how her actions will make other people feel. It seems that she believes her needs or wants are more important than anyone else's.

## Can You Hear What I'm Doing?

People usually say there are two types of communication: verbal and nonverbal. Verbal communication just

## THE IMPORTANCE OF EMPATHY

To see how important empathy is to society, you only need to look at some of our common expressions. You've probably heard the saying, "Walk a mile in someone else's shoes." That's just a way of talking about empathy. Or how about "Love they neighbor as thyself"? Or "Do unto others as you'd have them do unto you"? These are all really statements about empathy. When we understand how it feels to be in someone else's situation, it affects how we treat that person.

means talking—putting thoughts into words. Nonverbal communication involves things like facial expressions. If you ask a friend if she's okay, she might say, "Yeah, I'm fine." That's her verbal communication. But her nonverbal communication—the look on her face, the tone of her voice— might tell you the exact opposite.

But there's a third type of communication: behavior. Sometimes people act in a certain way because they can't find the words to say what is really on their minds. When adults talk about a child "acting out," that's what they mean. The child is upset about something, but he doesn't know how to explain himself, so he "flips out." The behavior of people with conduct disorder—even their really awful behavior—can be a strange form of communication.

It's not okay to hurt others because you can't say what you feel. People with conduct disorder are responsible for their choices, and they need to learn better social skills. But if someone in your life has conduct disorder, understanding that *behavior is communication* might help you cope. The person may be trying to express his own pain or anxiety, just in an unacceptable way.

Managing conduct disorder has a lot to do with this idea of communication. People with the disorder need to learn skills to express themselves in ways that are not so hurtful or destructive. In the next chapter, we'll talk about what can be done to get better.

**Famous writers have had a lot to say about empathy. In "Song of Myself" (1892), the poet Walt Whitman wrote, "I do not ask the wounded person how he feels, I become the wounded person."**

# ANXIETY AND DISRUPTIVE BEHAVIOR DISORDERS

From the outside, a person with a disruptive behavior disorder may just seem like a jerk. He's mean to people, he steals, he breaks things. If he has ODD, he may seem angry most of the time. He might even be violent.

It might surprise you to hear that many people who behave this way suffer from anxiety. They act tough, but they are actually very fearful on the inside. Maybe they worry about rejection—so instead of waiting to be rejected by others, they reject everyone else first. Maybe they are terrified of school—so they flip out whenever their teachers ask a simple question.

It's not uncommon for someone with a disruptive behavior disorder to also have some other problem. It can be anxiety, depression, bipolar disorder, or ADHD. These problems cause frustration, leading the person to act out in aggressive ways.

### Text-Dependent Questions

1. Name some social norms. Why are they important?
2. What are the symptoms of a conduct disorder?
3. What feelings are missing in people with conduct disorders?

### Research Project

Read your school's code of student conduct and think about the rules that are given. What social norms are being encouraged by those rules? They might include being on time, being honest, and being respectful of others. Write up some additional rules that you would like to see. What other social norms would *you* like to encourage?

# CHAPTER FOUR

# GETTING BETTER

**Words to Understand**

**alienate:** to drive someone away from you.

**cognitive:** having to do with the way we think.

**peer:** someone who is the same age or level as you.

The disorders in this book are different from anxiety, depression, and other mental disorders in a couple of important ways. The causes of behavior disorders tend to be a bit different, which means that the treatments differ as well.

## Causes

There is no simple answer to why behavior disorders happen. But they are probably caused by a few factors.

- **Biological factors**. People who have family members with mental disorders tend to be more likely to develop disorders themselves. Their brains may develop a bit differently. Or there might be a problem with their brain chemistry.

**If you grow up in a house with a lot of fighting, then shouting might seem "normal" to you. But that doesn't mean it's the best way to handle problems.**

- **Psychological factors**. Someone who has a negative relationship with his or her parents might be more likely to have a behavior disorder. Kids who have difficulty making friends might also be at risk.
- **Social factors.** A difficult home life could contribute to the problem, too. If someone's caregivers are neglectful or abusive, or if daily life feels unsafe or unstable, that might contribute to a behavior disorder. Even growing up poor could be a factor.

But these are just theories. None of these factors guarantee that a person will have a behavior disorder. There are plenty of people who have mentally ill relatives who never become ill themselves. Lots of people grow up poor and have no problems with behavior at all. Doctors think that a combination of the factors can trigger problems for specific people, but not for everyone.

Something else to notice about these factors is that most of them involve interactions with other people. This is where behavior disorders differ from, say, anxiety or depression. Someone with an anxiety disorder feels anxious no matter what else is happening. The same with depression: depressed people tend to feel sad most or all of the time. It doesn't matter what is happening on the outside—the problem is on the inside.

Behavior disorders are not like that. They involve interactions with other people. For that reason, doctors do not use the same treatments for behavior disorders that they might use for anxiety or depression.

**DID YOU KNOW?**

Behavior disorders are treatable. For example, if treated, about 67 percent of people with ODD have no symptoms within three years.

## MYTHS ABOUT ANGER

Sometimes when people feel anxious or insecure, they think that "acting tough" will fix the problem. The truth is, that rarely works. Aggression might get you what you want in the short term. But over time it will make you increasingly unhappy and alienate the people you care about.

Other people believe that anger is not controllable. They think that they have no choice but to express these feelings all the time, even if they hurt others. The truth is, there are useful ways to express negative feelings. Everybody feels angry sometimes, and that's fine. The question is, what do you do with those feelings? It is possible to learn techniques that will help you get along better with others.

### Treatments

There are a few types of treatments available for behavior disorders.

*Medication.* There is no pill that will make behavior disorders go away. But sometimes medication can help reduce the worst symptoms. This is especially true if the person has a behavior disorder along with another problem. For example, a kid who has ADHD and ODD might benefit a lot from medication. Some doctors also think that ADHD medication can help kids with conduct disorders.

*Cognitive-Behavioral Therapy (CBT).* The word cognitive refers to the thought process—what and how we think about ourselves and the world. In CBT, people learn to think about problems in different ways. For example, someone in CBT might practice the technique of counting to 10 before responding in an argument. Or someone might learn positive ways to respond to triggers. People with CBT also try to understand their disorder better. Having a behavior disorder does not make someone a bad person. CBT helps people learn to consciously make better choices.

*Family Therapy.* Behavior disorders have huge impacts on the families of people who have them. And, of course, caregivers are the ones in charge of punishing kids when they misbehave. So it's very important that families take part in therapy, to learn how to respond to behavior disorder symptoms in the most useful way. Some programs teach "parent management" techniques, which help parents do a better job at caring for their child.

*Social Skills Programs.* Similar to family therapy, these programs help kids learn how to get along better with their peers.

**Family therapy can help both parents and kids learn more productive ways to solve problems.**

## RESPONDING TO BEHAVIOR DISORDERS

Experts recommend that parents should strive for the following traits:

- **Be predictable**. What behaviors are or not okay should be clear to both parents and kids.
- **Be consistent**. If a certain behavior is not okay, that should be true all the time; it doesn't help if kids are allowed to act out at some times but not others.
- **Be reasonable**. Consequences should not be excessive; coming down super-hard on a misbehaving kid will probably not help.
- **Be supportive**. Reward good behavior with affection and praise; sometimes parents only notice when kids misbehave and overlook when they do things right.

Most treatments for behavior disorders involve learning how to make better choices. Let's look at a couple of themes that come up a lot.

### Adaptive versus Maladaptive Behavior

The word *adapt* means to adjust to a particular context. An adapter for a cell phone, for example, can make the phone able to play music through speakers.

When people talk about "adaptive behavior," they mean actions that help a person get along better in a particular situation. Saying "please" and "thank you" to your grandparents is adaptive behavior, because saying those things makes them happy. And pleasing your grandparents gets you things you want: a friendly visit, a good relationship with them, and possibly a gift.

**There is no cure in pill form for behavior disorders. However, medication can sometimes make people feel better for a short time, which can make them better able to work on their problems in therapy.**

The prefix *mal-* means "bad" or "poor." *Maladaptive* behaviors do not help a person get along, and in fact they make situations worse. Being rude to your grandparents is maladaptive behavior. It upsets your grandparents and makes them less likely to want to spend time with you. This is bad for the grandparents, and in the long run, it's bad for you, too.

But in the moment, someone with a behavior disorder may feel differently. She may have learned that the more difficult she is, the more likely she is to get what she needs. Over time, she has learned that she won't get it by a simple request—instead, parents and other adults have rewarded the bad behavior. Usually, this type of response—giving in to the bad behavior—is totally unintentional, but it happens anyway. It's a challenging interaction for everyone. And although both parent and child know there is a problem, they can't change the way they interact.

A big part of therapy involves learning what maladaptive behavior is and why it happens. The girl in our example can learn that there are lots of ways to express her feelings without being mean to Grandma. Meanwhile, Grandma learns new ways to manage challenging behavior.

## Anger Management

In earlier chapters, we talked about how people with behavior disorders can get extremely angry. Some people, especially those with conduct disorders, don't *feel* very angry, but they act out anyway. In either case, there are clearly a lot of negative emotions, and those emotions are being expressed in maladaptive ways. A type of therapy called "anger management" helps people learn how to cope with their negative feelings.

**Sometimes it helps to step away from an upsetting situation. Give yourself a few minutes to calm down and think about what is really bothering you.**

Anger management isn't just for people with behavior disorders. If you have ever taken a few deep breaths when you feel upset, you have tried a small form of anger management. The deep breaths create a pause—a brief space between the moment when something makes you feel angry and the moment when you respond. The pause gives you a chance to control what your response will be. Counting to 10 is another way to create that pause. It helps you stop, think about what you are doing, and make a better choice.

There are many other skills that anger management can teach. Many of them relate to understanding triggers. If you know in advance that certain situations make you upset, you can be prepared with a plan for what to do when it happens. Other anger management skills involve understanding consequences. What happens when you act out? Who is hurt

**Sometimes a person gets so upset, he loses control of his words or actions. At these moments, it¹s a good idea to take a step away from the person or situation that's so upsetting.**

and why? Answering these questions can help you be more aware of the choices you make.

## Taking Charge

We said earlier that disruptive behavior disorders are different from other mental disorders in certain ways. But in one sense, they are very similar.

A person with a behavior disorder has a problem, just like someone who has an anxiety disorder. And, for that matter, just like someone who has the flu. The disorder does not need to define the person. With help, people with behavior disorders can learn to make better choices. And these better choices will help them lead happier lives. It may feel sometimes like the angry, negative emotions are directing everything the person does. But it does not have to be that way. Negative feelings do not have to be in charge forever.

## Text-Dependent Questions

1. What are some possible causes of disruptive behavior disorders?
2. What is maladaptive behavior? Think of a few examples.
3. What is anger management, and how can it help people with behavior problems?

## Research Project

Learn more about anger management techniques. You might look for books in your library, or try web sites like the American Psychological Association (see the Further Reading section for the link). There are also storybooks that talk about how to cope with angry feelings. Make a list of tips for responding to anger and try them out the next time you get upset. Write about how the suggestions helped or did not help you.

"You are not your illness. You have an individual story to tell. You have a name, a history, a personality. Staying yourself is part of the battle."
—Julian Seifter

# Further Reading

## BOOKS

Drew, Naomi. *No Kidding About Bullying.* Minneapolis, MN: Free Spirit Publishing, 2010.

Greene, Ross W. *The Explosive Child: A New Approach for Understanding and Parenting Easily Frustrated, Chronically Inflexible Children.* 5th ed. New York: HarperCollins, 2014.

Quill, Charlie. *Anger and Anger Management.* New York: Rosen, 2008.

Riley, Douglas A. *The Defiant Child: A Parent's Guide to Oppositional Defiant Disorder.* Dallas: Taylor Trade Publishing, 1997.

## ONLINE

American Academy of Child and Adolescent Psychology. "Oppositional Defiant Disorder Resource Center." http://www.aacap.org/AACAP/Families_and_Youth/Resource_Centers/Oppositional_Defiant_Disorder_Resource_Center/Home.aspx.

American Psychological Association. "Controlling Anger Before It Controls You." http://www.apa.org/topics/anger/control.aspx.

Collingwood, Jane. "Dealing with Anger Constructively." *PsychCentral.* http://psychcentral.com/lib/dealing-with-anger-constructively/0003155.

Lives in the Balance. "Hope, Compassion, Support, and Help for Behaviorally Challenging Kids and Their Caregivers." http://www.livesinthebalance.org/LITB-mission.

Mind Tools. "Anger Management." http://www.mindtools.com/pages/article/newTCS_97.htm.

---

### LOSING HOPE?

This free, confidential phone number will connect you to counselors who can help.

**National Suicide Prevention Lifeline**
**1-800-273-TALK (1-800-273-8255)**

"Mental illness is nothing to be ashamed of, but stigma and bias shame us all. Together, we will replace stigma with acceptance, ignorance with understanding, fear with new hope for the future. Together, we will build a stronger nation for the new century, leaving no one behind."
—Bill Clinton

**Series Glossary**

**acute:** happening powerfully for a short period of time.

**affect:** as a noun, the way someone seems on the outside—including attitude, emotion, and voice (pronounced with the emphasis on the first syllable, "AFF-eckt").

**atypical:** different from what is usually expected.

**bipolar:** involving two, opposite ends.

**chronic:** happening again and again over a long period of time.

**comorbidity:** two or more illnesses appearing at the same time.

**correlation:** a relationship or connection.

**delusion:** a false belief with no connection to reality.

**dementia:** a mental disorder, featuring severe memory loss.

**denial:** refusal to admit that there is a problem.

**depressant:** a substance that slows down bodily functions.

**depression:** a feeling of hopelessness and lack of energy.

**deprivation:** a hurtful lack of something important.

**diagnose:** to identify a problem.

**empathy:** understanding someone else's situation and feelings.

**epidemic:** a widespread illness.

**euphoria:** a feeling of extreme, even overwhelming, happiness.

**hallucination:** something a person sees or hears that is not really there.

**heredity:** the passing of a trait from parents to children.

**hormone:** a substance in the body that helps it function properly.

**hypnotic:** a type of drug that causes sleep.

**impulsivity:** the tendency to act without thinking.

**inattention:** distraction; not paying attention.

**insomnia:** inability to fall asleep and/or stay asleep.

**licensed:** having an official document proving one is capable with a certain set of skills.

**manic:** a high level of excitement or energy.

**misdiagnose:** to incorrectly identify a problem.

**moderation:** limited in amount, not extreme.

**noncompliance:** refusing to follow rules or do as instructed.

**onset:** the beginning of something; pronounced like "on" and "set."

**outpatient:** medical care that happens while a patient continues to live at home.

**overdiagnose:** to determine more people have a certain illness than actually do.

**pediatricians:** doctors who treat children and young adults.

**perception:** awareness or understanding of reality.

**practitioner:** a person who actively participates in a particular field.

**predisposition:** to be more likely to do something, either due to your personality or biology.

**psychiatric:** having to do with mental illness.

**psychiatrist:** a medical doctor who specializes in mental disorders.

**psychoactive:** something that has an effect on the mind and behavior.

**psychosis:** a severe mental disorder where the person loses touch with reality.

**psychosocial:** the interaction between someone's thoughts and the outside world of relationships.

**psychotherapy:** treatment for mental disorders.

**relapse:** getting worse after a period of getting better.

**spectrum:** a range; in medicine, from less extreme to more extreme.

**stereotype:** a simplified idea about a type of person, not connected to actual individuals.

**stimulant:** a substance that speeds up bodily functions.

**therapy:** treatment of a problem; can be done with medicine or simply by talking with a therapist.

**trigger:** something that causes something else.

# Index

Page numbers in *italics* refer to photographs.

## About the Author

**H. W. POOLE** is a writer and editor of books for young people, such as the *Horrors of History* series (Charlesbridge). She is also responsible for many critically acclaimed reference books, including *Political Handbook of the World* (CQ Press) and the *Encyclopedia of Terrorism* (SAGE). She was coauthor and editor of the *History of the Internet* (ABC-CLIO), which won the 2000 American Library Association RUSA award.

## About the Advisor

**ANNE S. WALTERS** is Clinical Associate Professor of Psychiatry and Human Behavior. She is the Clinical Director of the Children's Partial Hospital Program at Bradley Hospital, a program that provides partial hospital level of care for children ages 7–12 and their families. She also serves as Chief Psychologist for Bradley Hospital. She is actively involved in teaching activities within the Clinical Psychology Training Programs of the Alpert Medical School of Brown University and serves as Child Track Seminar Co-Coordinator. Dr. Walters completed her undergraduate work at Duke University, graduate school at Georgia State University, internship at UTexas Health Science Center, and postdoctoral fellowship at Brown University. Her interests lie in the area of program development, treatment of severe psychiatric disorders in children, and psychotic spectrum disorders.

## Photo Credits

*Photos are for illustrative purposes only; individuals depicted in the photos, both on the cover and throughout this book, are only models.*

**Cover Photo:** Dollar Photo Club/vectorass

**Dollar Photo Club:** 10 Ilike; 13 inna_astakhova; 15 highwaystarz; 16 bramgino; 19 diego cervo; 20 olly; 21 Robert Kneschke; 22 taramara78; 25 Fotosenmeer.nl; 26 kokotewan; 28 VIPDesign; 33 doble.d; 36 Lisa F. Young; 38 18percentgrey; 39 pavelkriuchkov; 40 ladybirdstudio. **Library of Congress:** 30.